PERSONAL FINANCE: THE COMPLETE BEGINNER'S GUIDE

A SIMPLE PRACTICAL APPROACH TO MAKING MONEY, SAVING, & INVESTING

BY CRAIG SANTORO

Published by:

ALEX-PUBLISHING

Table of Contents

Authors Note:

Somebody once said that failing to plan is planning to fail. And failing to manage is managing to fail. Just like an untended garden, many important areas of our lives can be very messy to say the least without good active management. One of those areas is personal finance.

We all have needs and wants, which all require money. Personal finance is the ongoing activity of managing our money so that we can ensure that all our needs – both current and future ones – are met along with as much of our wants as possible.

Most people get by meeting their current needs and leave the future ones to fate. We shouldn't do that. We should prepare for them while we still have time. Personal finance management can go a long way in helping us prepare to meet our future needs like retirement or our children's college education.

In this book, you will learn about several of the key building blocks of Personal Finance; Cash Flow Management, Saving and Investing. I will show you how to achieve positive cash flows as a means to meet both current and future needs. You will learn how to properly save and ways in which to beat inflation through properly investing your money. Finally, you will learn how to properly consider investments based on your objectives, risk tolerance, average expected rates of return, average inflation rate and time frame. For this, I will teach you to carefully and wisely evaluate you investment alternatives.

Actively managing your personal finances will enable you meet your needs, have some for wants, help others and provide a greater degree of peace of mind. This book was written in a way that can be easily understood using examples from everyday living and is a very good springboard for learning more advanced personal finance topics.

Best,

Craig Santoro

"Many people take no care of their money till they come nearly to the end of it, and others do just the same with their time."

– Johann Wolfgang von Goethe

INTRODUCTION

Money does make your world go round. Beg to disagree? Consider the best things in life that are supposedly free:

-A great marriage;

-Deep relationships;

-Peace of mind; and

-Giving to churches and charitable organizations.

You can't have a great marriage without money, at least enough of it. How many marriages have fallen apart because the inability to meet physical and financial needs have caused so much stress? You can't take your wife to dinner or a romantic getaway without money. You can't dress up well for your husband if you don't have money for clothes. You won't have time for your spouse if you're too busy trying to make ends meet.

You also can't have meaningful relationships with other people without money. Texting people require money. If you think connecting through Facebook is free, it isn't - you need money to buy a gadget and to avail of Internet connection. It also takes money to go out and spend quality time with friends. As with marriage, you can't really spend quality time with them if you're too preoccupied trying to make ends meet.

When you're honest with yourself, you'll agree that to a great extent, money is key to having peace of mind. It's easy to say God provides when you're not in need. But when you're neck-deep in debt and you don't have money to pay for this month's rent, you'll probably be singing a different tune.

Lastly, no matter how much you want to finance the great work your church or your favorite charitable organization is doing, you can't do that without extra money. If you aren't able to provide for your needs, how can you provide for others'?

If you're ready to start successfully managing your personal finances, turn the page and let's go!

PERSONAL FINANCE 101

"Many people take no care of their money till they come nearly to the end of it, and others do just the same with their time." – Johann Wolfgang von Goethe

Now that's a very good point to consider – taking care of money. Why should we take care of our money? Isn't money supposed to take care of us? I mean, that's why we – as Donna Summer sang – work hard for the money, right?

Yes, money is supposed to take care of us – our needs and wants. But money can't take care of itself. Like a puppet that's manipulated for the entertainment pleasure of the audience, so is money controlled for our purposes. It's something that needs to be actively controlled to enjoy the benefits. And this is where personal finance management comes in.

Personal finance management is basically the art and science of managing money in order to ensure that our needs are met. If you'd like to include wants in the definition, feel free to do so. At the core, however, personal finance management is about meeting needs so even if you're not able to meet some or most of your wants, you still managed your personal finances well.

But then again, we all want some life sweeteners now, don't we?

For purposes of personal finance management, we can classify our needs according to time: current and future.

Current needs are obviously those that need to be met now and on a regular basis such as food, clothing, shelter, transportation, electricity, water and for some, medicines. Future ones include the tuition fees of our children once they are of age to study, medical and hospital expenses in the event of an unexpected medical condition that will require being confined and retirement.

Most people think they're already doing a good job of managing their personal finances because they're still alive, which means they're able to meet their needs even if it's just getting by. But if we consider the primary goal of personal finance management, which is to meet all needs, as well as the kind of needs, we'll find that meeting current needs doesn't make for successfully managing our finances. Successfully managing our finances including being able to address future needs at least to a great extent.

THE RIGHT TIME

There's a saying that haste makes waste. It may be true for many things but not potential matters of life and death. I mean, what would you think of me if I told the driver of an ambulance carrying a person who figured in serious car accident to drive slowly because haste makes waste? Right! You'd say I was nuts for applying a principle outside it's true context. It's the same with personal finances. Haste minimizes or prevents waste.

What kind of waste are we talking about here? First of all, time. Unlike wasted money, which can be earned again, wasted time is gone forever. We can't recoup the losses.

Another waste is opportunity. As David Bolyard once said: "Seize the moment for some opportunities don't come twice." What are some of these opportunities?

The first opportunity we'll miss by delaying personal finance management is a lighter savings and investment burden. What do we mean by this? When we start saving and investing earlier than later, we'll have more time to save and invest for our future needs, which means the amount of money we need to save and invest regularly is less compared to starting later. Consider 2 simple mathematical examples:

$100 ÷ 10 years = $10/year

$100 ÷ 5 years = $20/year

Do you see how our financial burden can be lessened when we have a longer time to save up and invest for future needs, which is possible when we start managing our personal finances as early as possible?

Another opportunity we can miss by delaying personal finance management is being able to successfully meet a future need. Why? One of the biggest reasons is inflation, which is the rate at which prices of our needs increase. Strictly speaking, inflation rate is a number computed by economists, which tell us how much the prices of basic commodities have gone up in the last 12 months. A published inflation rate of 5% for last month for example, means that the basic costs of living went up by 5% on average from the same month last year.

What does it have to do with missing the opportunity to provide for future needs? Say you want to have your own house by the time you retire in 10 years and that the average price of a decent home these days is $100,000.00. This means you'll have to save and invest at least $10,000 annually. But because the prices of houses, as with most other things, continue to go up every year, the money you would've saved by the time you retired in 10 years ($100,000) will no longer be enough because the average prices of decent homes by then would've gone up significantly due to inflation. When you manage your personal finances well, you get the opportunity to either have enough money to buy a decent house in by the time you retire or be able to lock in on the price of houses now even if you don't have the money yet.

Another future need – one that's sure to come up – is retirement. Consider your average monthly living expenses today and multiply it by the number of months you expect to live after retiring. The total amount you arrived at won't be the actual amount you'll need – you'll need much more because of inflation. By the time you retire, the average cost of living will be significantly higher. Personal finance management can help you take care of that.

ACCRUAL AND CASH CONCEPTS

One relatively technical thing we'll need to get a good grasp of when it comes to personal finance management is the concepts of accrual and cash method of recording financial transactions. Let's talk about the accrual method first.

Under the accrual method of recording financial transactions, income is recorded or recognized as they are earned, not when they are received. Expenses, on the other hand, are recorded as they are incurred, not when they are paid out. What does this mean in layman's terms?

Let's say you're an engineer and you earn a living as a private practitioner. After completing a project, you are now entitled to your pay as stated in your contract or agreement with your client. Under the accrual method, you already record the income now because you already earned it, i.e., you now have a valid legal claim to such money because you already completed the agreed upon service. So your income for this month would reflect the pay from this project.

Under the cash method however, you won't record it as income just yet because you haven't received the payment. If the client pays you next month, only then will you record it as income.

As for expenses, consider your monthly electric bill. When you receive your billing statement, it's usually payable on a certain date in the future. You're given a grace period from the time you're billed to the time you pay the amount. Under the accrual method, you already record it as an expense for the current period because you already have a valid legal obligation to pay the amount, even if it's in the future. Under the cash method however, you record it as an expense for the particular period wherein you actually pay for it.

So what's the big deal about the different methods? Income and expenses will be recorded either way so why do we need to be aware of both? The reason: liquidity.

Liqui-what? Liquidity refers to our ability to meet our financial obligations as they fall due. Personal finance is about liquidity because we need money, not claims to money, to pay for our needs and wants. Let me illustrate.

For simplicity's sake, let's assume you only have one source of income – consultancy services – and only one expense – apartment rental. Further, let's assume you earned $1,500 from being a company's consultant but the terms of conditions of that engagement state that you'll be paid on the 2nd Monday of the following month. The rental on your apartment, however, is due at the end of the current month. Even if your income is 2 times your monthly rental, it won't mean much if you don't get it on time in order to pay the rent.

The risk with using the accrual method for recording and planning is that it doesn't take into consideration the timing of receipt and spending of cash. Using the accrual method for the above-mentioned example, you may think you're doing well because income significantly exceeds expense for the month but it doesn't tell you that you don't have the money to pay for the expense during the period. The cash method of recording and planning allows you to minimize your liquidity risk or the risk that you won't be able to meet your financial obligations. You'll appreciate this concept better in Chapter 2 on cash flow management.

TIME VALUE OF MONEY

One of the cornerstones of personal finance management is the concept of the time value of money, which states that our money that's available now is worth more than the same amount in the future because of the opportunity to make it grow. To put it another way, we'd be better off receiving, say, $100 now instead of $100 a year from now because we have the opportunity to make the money grow between now and 12 months later. This is the reason for charging interest on borrowed money and earning money from investments, particularly from lending money. This concept is the foundation for investing as well as debts.

OVERVIEW

The rest of this book will be dedicated to helping you meet your current and future needs by teaching you how to manage your finances properly through cash flow management (including budgeting), debt management, saving and investing your savings well. I will explain these concepts to you in a simple and straightforward manner so that you'll be able to really grasp these key concepts and help you understand more advanced personal finance reading materials later on.

CASH FLOW MANAGEMENT

"The fact is that one of the earliest lessons I learned in business was that balance sheets and income statements are fiction. Cash flow is reality." – Chris Chocola

Money moves in 2 ways: into our accounts or wallets and away from them. These movements are called cash flows and when it comes to ensuring our current and future needs are met, this is the key that'll spell success or failure in terms of personal finance management.

Why is that so? Remember liquidity or the ability to meet financial obligations when they fall due? It's dependent on how much cash we have and that is dependent on how we manage our cash flows. When we allow more money to move away from us compared to what moves into our accounts and wallets, our liquidity is compromised.

INFLOWS, OUTFLOWS AND POSITIONS

Events that move cash into our accounts and wallets are called cash inflows while those that move cash out from our accounts and wallets are called cash outflows. Examples of cash inflows are salaries, cash gifts and cash prizes won. Examples of cash outflows include bills payment, donating to a charitable institution, buying clothes or giving tithes and offerings in church.

If our cash inflows exceed outflows during a certain period, we experience what is called a positive cash flow position. When cash outflows exceed cash inflows, we are in a negative cash flow position. When both are equal, we have a square or neutral position.

Neutral positions mean that we are only able to meet current needs and without any surplus or savings, we won't be able to set anything aside for future needs. It also increases our liquidity risk – the possibility that we won't be able to meet our financial obligations – because if something happens to us that'll negatively affect our cash inflows, we don't have any savings or buffer to cover cash outflows.

Negative cash positions obviously mean we aren't able to meet current needs at all. Aside from failing to meet our current needs, being in a consistent state of negative cash flows every month will bury us deep in bad debts, which we'll discuss further in Chapter 3. Suffice to say, this can become a downward spiral of increasing bad debts and eventually, bankruptcy.

The ideal cash position is a positive one, which means we're not just able to meet current needs but we're also able to put aside money to provide for future ones. Unfortunately, consistent positive cash flows aren't easy to do because human nature gravitates toward spending as much money as is available. Enjoying positive cash flows may require a great deal of discipline and consistency to achieve but it's well worth it.

MAXIMIZING CASH INFLOWS

To maximize cash inflows, we need to identify 2 sources: recurring and non-recurring. Recurring sources – those that regularly provide cash inflows – include your job, business, certain types of investments and for some people, allowances from parents or companies. These sources are crucial to meeting our current needs because they offer a great degree of stability and consistency. Because current needs are recurring, most of our cash inflows should also be from recurring sources.

Non-recurring sources include work bonuses that are contingent on our personal and the company's performance, cash gifts, proceeds of sales of personal assets and occasional side income. We shouldn't rely on these for current needs because as we said, stability and consistency is key to meeting such needs and these neither stable nor consistent. These are good for complementing recurring sources, especially for saving up and investing for future needs.

One key to maximizing cash inflows is by establishing as many sources of recurring income as possible, also known by a more technical term called diversification. Basically, we don't want to put all our eggs in one basket, just in case that basket falls. By having several sources of recurring cash inflows, we lower the risk for disrupted cash inflows.

Another key to maximizing cash inflows is to establish recurring sources that are passive. Passive recurring income sources are those that require minimal active involvement in order to generate cash. In other words, these are sources that you can pretty much leave alone to produce cash inflows. Because these sources don't require much of your time and attention, you can set up more recurring sources of cash inflows and thus maximize them. We'll talk more about passive sources of recurring income – also known as passive investments – in Chapter 5.

MINIMIZING CASH OUTFLOWS

Maximizing cash inflows can only go so far and the biggest chunk of successfully managing our personal finances is accounted for by cash outflows. In fact, no amount of cash inflows will ever be enough if we don't rein in our cash outflows. Consider the following celebrities who have amassed fortunes that can comfortably sustain many family generations without having to work a single day of their lives but still ended up bankrupt:

-Michael Jackson: The King Of Pop, whose reported earnings reached more than $1.0 billion in his entire career died with more debts than assets or bankrupt.

-Allen Iverson: This NBA superstar who was a 1-time MVP awardee from the Philadelphia 76ers earned a whopping $154 million throughout his career only to go bankrupt in 2012.

-Tony Braxton: Best known for the classic hit Un-Break My Heart and Breathe Again, this sultry singer went bankrupt twice – in 1998 and 2010. This despite her multi-million dollar hit singles and concerts that were always sold out.

The belief that the solution to life's problems is simply more money is dead wrong. True, more money helps but without controlling cash outflows, more money can actually mean more problems. Just ask the above-mentioned celebrities.

As with cash inflows, it's best to understand which of our cash outflows are recurring and non-recurring. Recurring cash outflows include food, transportation expenses, electricity, recreation, medical expenses and children's education. Non-recurring ones include travel expenses (for most people whose businesses and careers don't involve international or even domestic travel), housewarming gifts, purchases of furniture, buying appliances and hospitalization.

More than segregating them into recurring and non-recurring, it's also important to classify them either as needs or wants. Needs obviously have to be met and should take priority over wants but problems often arise when we justify wants as needs. Take for example, smartphones. We can actually live without one but because everyone has it, we don't want to be left out and so we feel we need it to survive. Just ask a teenager to give up their smartphone and you will effectively declare the beginning of World War III! Granted that it really is considered a necessity these days, we simply need one to make and receive calls and messages. That's it. We don't really need to get the latest top-of-the-line smartphones that cost as much as most people's 2-months' salaries in 3rd world countries.

I can't over-emphasize the necessity of correctly classifying needs vs. wants, especially if we don't belong to the upper or even middle class. Take the example of a person I know who I shall henceforth name as Joker. Joker, despite not finishing high school or college, has managed to get a fairly good-paying job as a call center agent. As such, he was finally able live on his own and provide for most of his personal needs. But then the smartphone bug bit him and though he can't afford an iPhone, he borrowed money to buy one. The payment terms, however, were too heavy for him and it wasn't long before he defaulted. He had to sell the phone at a much lower price and the proceeds weren't even enough to pay for the loan. Worse, he got cut from his job and because he didn't have any savings, he had to give up his pad, go back to his parents and was unable to provide for his personal needs.

So how can we minimize or reduce our cash outflows? Here are several ways:

-Un-brand: Many of the things we regularly consume have lower-priced alternative brands and the higher price tag of top brands doesn't necessarily mean significantly better quality. There's no guilt or shame in going for cheaper brands but there is when we file for bankruptcy because of stubbornly holding on to expensive brands that we can't really afford.

-Super-Size It: Buying supplies in bulk helps save money and reduce cash outflows. How? First, buying in bulk saves us quite a number of trips to the grocery, which helps us reduce gasoline or commuting expenses. Second, most manufacturers sell bigger-sized versions at significantly lower prices that can add up to significant savings.

-Flee From Temptations: Many times, we find ourselves spending so much for unnecessary things because we put ourselves in a position to be tempted to do so. We know that there's a big sale at the mall, which makes un-planned splurges very enticing, but still go there anyway. We end up justifying the splurges as "too good to resist" and "great steals". The great theft really was on us because we didn't really need to buy those things in the first place. We should avoid places and situations that we know can cause us to splurge on unnecessary things and we significantly reduce our cash outflows.

-The Company We Keep: Similar to tempting situations are people who splurge without thinking. Hanging with such people can force us to spend more than we can afford just to keep up. Avoiding such a crowd can go a long way in helping us minimize the temptation to spend unnecessarily and reduce or minimize our cash outflows.

-Education: Private schools can sometimes be way too overrated as to quality of education to the point that people who can't afford to send their kids to such schools are forced to get into bad debts just to do so. When you consider the best schools in the country, some of them are public. The schools children go to can only go so far when it comes to their success – the bigger slice of the pie are their attitudes and study habits. There's no shame in sending our children to good public schools but there is when we go bankrupt and our children stop going to school as a result.

-Contentment: Possibly the single biggest factor when it comes to minimizing cash outflows, contentment is a virtue that's almost extinct. Why? We live in a society that glorifies self and actually promotes discontent – you have to have more because you deserve more! To get an idea just how discontent people these days can be and how fatal it can be financially, look no further than the 2008 United States sub-prime mortgage crisis. Financial institutions stirred up the greed in the hearts of many homeowners. Why be content with just one house and why not borrow to buy more, even if you can't afford it? Because of greed, many people got into mortgages without reading the fine print and when the rates adjusted, many of them defaulted that lead to one of the worst financial crises ever recorded in the history of mankind. When we're content, we cut way down on unnecessary spending and maximize the benefits of our cash inflows.

THE KEY TO SUCCESSFUL CASH FLOW MANAGEMENT

Budgeting is our secret weapon when it comes to successful cash flow management. Why? Because budgeting allows us to see our true financial position and allows us to exercise a great deal of control over it. Think of it this way – it's like riding a bike uphill. When we don't do anything and let nature take its course, we'll slide down backwards and may even fall down as a result. But when we take control of the bike by pedaling, balancing and when necessary, apply the brakes, we can successfully reach the top. With personal finance, budgeting is akin to pedaling, balancing and braking our bikes to reach the top of the hill.

So how do we exactly go about budgeting? There are 3 steps: know, plan and execute.

In the knowing stage, we need to get an accurate estimate of our average monthly cash inflows and outflows. The extent to which we can accurately estimate these is the extent to which we can successfully plan our budget.

Do you have an idea of how much you spend and make on a monthly basis? If you don't, there are several ways to estimate your monthly cash inflows and outflows. Estimating cash inflows is very simple, especially if you're employed. If you're an entrepreneur, you can either get the figures from your business' accounting records or your previous year's tax return.

The quickest and simplest way of estimating your average monthly cash outflows is by reviewing your credit card and other billing statements for the last 6 months. This can give you a good estimate of your average monthly cash outflows. But since this doesn't factor in other expenses that aren't included in your statements of accounts like your regular lunches at your favorite hotdog stand across the street or your daily commuting expenses, you can either estimate those regular expenses and add them to your initial estimates or simply add a buffer of 10% to 20% to the initial one.

Once you know your average monthly cash position (positive, negative or neutral), you can plan on how to adjust accordingly to meet your needs, whether current or future. If you find that you're monthly cash position is often neutral or negative, you can look at ways to increase your cash inflows, reduce your cash outflows or both. You'll need to be realistic with your plans though, taking into consideration the average increases or decreases in certain sources or uses of your money. For example, planning to slash your food expenses by 50% starting next month may be unachievable considering that the current amount you spend on food isn't enough to keep you from feeling hungry most of the time. Another unrealistic plan would be increasing your salary by 50% when on the average, your employer gives a salary increase of only 10% at best and only 5% on average every year.

Lastly, even the best-laid plans are of no value unless executed well. You should focus and be disciplined enough to execute your budget plan. Without focus and discipline, it'll be practically impossible to implement a budget plan well.

PERSONAL DEBT MANAGEMENT

"Debt is like a very sharp kitchen knife. Handled expertly with care, it's an instrument of delight. Otherwise, it can seriously hurt you." – Seph Romana, Financial Literacy Advocate

If debt were a character, it's got to be one of the most misunderstood and vilified. If it were a defendant in court, he or she is already guilty until proven innocent. Why? It's because many people have been wrecked financially because of debt – and that's true! That however, isn't enough reason to crucify personal debt like the ancient Romans did. As Seph Romana said, the way it's handled determines whether we'll experience delight or hurt.

DEBT 101

In personal finance, debt is the legal obligation to pay somebody or some institution an amount of money. Debt arises from borrowing money or as a consequence of an action such as when we accidentally hurt someone or damage his or her possessions. In most cases, debt isn't a criminal offense but in many jurisdictions, purposefully running away from such – like changing addresses without notifying the person or institution to which money is owed – is considered as such.

In debt, the commodity in question isn't money but the privilege of using other people's money for a period of time. It's a privilege because we don't have the legal right to use others' money without their permission in the same manner we can't just take off with our neighbors' cars and expect them to be jubilant about it. As with all other commodities, debt has a price tag – interest.

INTEREST

Interest – expressed as percent (%) per annum (year) – is the benefit we give to the owners of the money we borrow in exchange for allowing us to use their money. It compensates them for passing on the opportunity to use their money to make more money when they lend it to us. It's sad to hear of many people – personal finance gurus included – to talk about interest as some despicable abomination of desolation. If that were the case, we should be condemning our friendly neighborhood grocery store owner for adding to the cost of their merchandise when they sell it to us. But we don't because we know it's only fair as a business practice to do so, right? Right!

Different debt sources have different interest rates and the one thing they have in common is that their rates reflect the riskiness of the loans they extend. This is known as credit risk or the possibility that the debt can't be repaid by the borrower. The riskier the debt, the higher the interest rate charged.

Credit cards usually charge the highest interest rates. Why? Because apart from being the riskier type of debt for lenders, it's also meant for payment convenience and not as a form of financial assistance. Credit card companies intentionally set high interest rates to encourage people to pay their bills on time and discourage using credit cards as financial support.

Loan sharks also charge some of the, if not the highest interest rates because of the very high risks they take to lend money. Most of the people who come to them are desperate, i.e., rejected by most traditional lending institutions due to their dire financial positions. Their financial position plus the fact that most loan sharks don't require collateral only magnifies the credit risk they take when lending.

Traditional lending institutions like banks charge some of the lowest if not the least interest, especially if the loan is secured by a collateral, e.g., properties and vehicles. They also tend to be very tedious in terms of documentation and establishing our credit worthiness, which significantly lowers their credit risk and consequently, interest rates charged.

How is interest computed? Here's the formula:

$$\text{Interest} = P \times I \times \left[\frac{t}{360 \text{ or } 12}\right]$$

Where: P = Principal amount owed;

    I = Interest rate charged;

    t = time expressed in actual # of days or months; and

    360 if t is in days and 12 if t is in months.

Say we borrowed $100 for 6 months at 10% interest rate. The price we'll have to pay for the privilege of using someone else's money (interest) would be:

Interest = $100 x 10% x [6/12]

Interest = $100 x 10% x 0.5

Interest = $5

Given all things equal, the shorter is the duration of our loan, the lower our interest will be and vice versa.

THE POWER OF COMPOUNDING

"Compound interest is the 8th wonder of the world. He who understands it, earns it. He who doesn't, pays it." – Albert Einstein

In layman's terms, compounding is a process by which any interest owed or income due is added back to the principal to become the new (and higher) principal for the next loan or investment period. If renew the loan in the above-mentioned example for another 6 months, the new principal will be higher at $105 and consequently, so will the interest payment be at $5.25.

When it comes to compounding, another critical component aside from the interest rate is the compounding frequency or the number of times interest is computed. Remember this: Given the same interest rate, the more frequently we compound, the greater will our interest be. Why? Consider the difference in interest when we borrow $10,000 for 1 year compounded quarterly (4 times) and annually (once) at 10% per year.

Compounded Quarterly

	Beginning Principal	Interest	Ending Principal
1st Quarter	$10,000.00	$250.00	$10,250.00
2nd Quarter	$10,250.00	$256.25	$10,506.25
3rd Quarter	$10,506.25	$262.66	$10,768.91
4th Quarter	$10,768.91	$269.22	$11,038.13

Total interest for the loan that we compounded quarterly is $1,038.13[1].

If compounded annually, the interest will just be $1,000.00. Now, a $38 difference may not mean much but consider if the loan is for 10 years. Total interest for the loan compounded quarterly and annually will be $16,850.64 (click here to see how we arrived at the figure) and $15,937.42 (click here to see how we arrived at the figure) or a difference of $913.21, which is now quite a significant amount, isn't it?

LUMP SUM OR INSTALLMENT?

There are 2 ways to pay off our debts: through a series of principal and interest payments (installments) or with a single payment of both the principal and interest at the end of the loan period (lump sum). Which is the more beneficial way of paying? It depends.

A lump sum payment scheme will be more beneficial for us if the cash inflow we expect that will pay for it will come towards the end of the loan period. Further, we can maximize the use of borrowed money with this payment scheme. The downside however, is higher interest (click here to see why).

With an installment payment scheme, we pay less interest because of lower principal for succeeding compounding periods as you saw in Appendix C. The disadvantage is we may not be able to maximize the money because we'll have to pay part of it back every month, quarter or compounding period.

TO BORROW OR NOT TO BORROW? THAT IS THE QUESTION

A simple question indeed, though one that's not as simple to answer. A wrong answer can mean the difference between prosperity and poverty, abundance and bankruptcy. It's therefore important to think well about whether or not to borrow money.

The first criterion is necessity. Do we really need to borrow money? If not, we shouldn't, even if we can afford to pay it back.

Why? Debt is like prescription drugs – it can be very addicting. Like such drugs, they're best used sparingly – only when needed. Once debt becomes a habit, it's hard to break and can have very serious financial consequences. But when we really need the money, especially if it's a matter of life and death situation, borrowing money is definitely a yes!

The second criterion is affordability. Can we afford to pay it back given the payment terms and conditions? If we need to borrow money and we can afford to pay it back, then it's good to borrow money. Consider the purchase of a family house.

I grew up in a middle class family, with both my parents working hard and being financially responsible. When they first got married, they lived with my grandparents, first from my mom's side then from my dad's. After a while, living with them no longer became an option – we needed to move out. At that time, my folks didn't have enough money to buy a house. They didn't want to rent for the rest of their lives either. And as much as they wanted to save up for a house, the rate at which the average prices of houses increase annually was much faster than their ability to save. So what did they do?

They borrowed money from the bank to purchase our family house. They paid it off in monthly installments for 20 years at terms and conditions that their respective cash flows can comfortably afford. Boy, am I glad they borrowed money to buy our house. Today, the market value of our home has gone up by at least 2,000% in the last 30 years since they bought it. Had they waited to save, they would've missed the opportunity to have our own family house. We could've been stuck with my grandparents...or be living off the streets.

Another criterion to consider when borrowing money is profitability. Borrowing money can actually increase a business' return on investment. By borrowing money, we need less of our own money to fund a business. Yes, net income may go down because of interest expense but because borrowing requires significantly less money from us, we can enjoy a higher return on investment. Click here to see how this is so.

Another criterion for borrowing is matching cash flows. What do I mean by this? There will be times that the money we expect to receive may come in much later than when we have to pay them out. Borrowing money helps us bridge that gap, to tide us over so to speak, until we receive the expected cash.

Say for example, we're in the trading business and most of the establishments that carry our goods require a 60-day window, i.e., they'll only pay us for the merchandise 60 days after receiving them. If our own suppliers give us a much shorter window, say only 30 days for the merchandise we purchased from them, how will we be able to pay in 30 days when our own customers will only pay us on the 60th day?

This is where borrowing money makes very good business sense. We have very low credit risk because we're just borrowing money only until the money we expect to receive comes. We're just advancing the money we already know is on the way.

WHEN TO AVOID PERSONAL DEBT

My answer to that question is...as much as possible and whenever possible. Why? As I mentioned earlier, it can be addicting so it's best to limit personal debt to when it's really needed.

Another reason is that unlike business debts, particularly those of a corporation's, we are personally liable for the money we owe, which means our personal properties or possessions may be affected by our creditors' claims. Corporations have a separate legal identity from those of its owners and as such, corporate debts are limited merely to the corporation's assets. Sole proprietorships' and partnerships' (except for limited life companies or LLCs) owners are also personally liable for debts by the business.

Do not borrow money to buy depreciable consumer items like smartphones, tablets or even vehicles. It's because their values immediately plunge by about 20% to 30% as soon as you take them home from the store or dealership and if you suddenly find yourself needing money, selling them will get you way less money than what you paid for. Further, these are the types of debt-funded items that make borrowing money such a hard addiction to break and have been the cause of downfall for many people. If you really need to, purchase good second hand ones when possible.

GETTING OUT OF BAD PERSONAL DEBTS

Getting out of bad personal debts, even if we're buried neck-deep in it, is possible. All we need is a lot of discipline and financial wisdom.

If consistent negative cash flows are the reason for being buried in bad personal debts, then the solution is to achieve consistent positive cash flows, i.e., more inflows than outflows.

To do this, we'll need to determine how much is our total debts. After that, we'll need to determine how much is the minimum amount we need to pay monthly to start reducing the amount of debt we have. The more we exceed this amount, the faster we can pay off our debts.

After determining the minimum amount, we'll need to determine if it's something our monthly cash flows can afford. If it isn't we need to seriously consider increasing cash inflows, minimizing cash outflows or both. We can refer to the tips in Chapter 3 on how to maximize cash inflows and minimize cash outflows.

If it's something we can afford, let's still consider increasing inflows and reducing outflows because as we said, the bigger the amount that we can pay every month, the faster we can reduce our bad personal debts and get out.

If after doing everything we can to maximize inflows and minimize outflows, we still can't afford to pay the minimum monthly amount needed to continuously reduce our personal debts, we need to consider selling personal assets to bring it down to an amount that would significantly bring down the minimum required monthly payments.

If all else fails, we should consider talking to our creditors to restructure our debts. It's highly unlikely they'll turn us down because restructuring will increase their chances of being able to recover the money that they lent. Asking to restructure is also a sign of goodwill, that we're willing to pay our debts.

HOW TO STAY OUT OF BAD PERSONAL DEBTS

Staying out of bad personal debts is relatively simple though it may be quite difficult, especially in this day and age of gadget lust and I-need-to-have-it-all attitude. Here are ways on how to stay out of bad personal debts:

-Contentment: Many times, it's lack of this virtue that buries people in bad personal debts. When we're content, we have less "needs" to finance. We don't need to indulge in luxuries that we can't afford to pay in cash, at least not without compromising other real needs. Being content may require work, because society today screams that being content isn't good. Fight for it. It'll be worth it.

-Company We Keep: It's been said that birds of the same feather flock together. I also believe that if you hang around certain birds, you start to grown the same feathers. It's best to stay clear of people who spend like there's no tomorrow on many unnecessary and frivolous things especially if we don't have as much cash as they do.

-Live Below Our Means: Yes, you read that right. We shouldn't live within our means, it's best to live below it. Merely living within our means may not allow us to save money for potential rainy days but living below our means can.

-Learn: Knowledge is power and the more we learn about personal finance management, the more we'll want to and learn how to avoid falling into the pitfalls of bad personal debt and if ever we'll borrow money, we'll be able to manage it wisely.

---

[1] $11,038.13 – $10,000.00

SAVING MONEY

"All days are not the same. Save for a rainy day. When you don't work, savings will work for you." – M. K. Soni

In Chapter 1, we defined personal finance management as a process whose goal is to be able to provide for current and future needs. In order to provide for future needs, we need to consistently be in a state of positive cash flows, i.e., more cash flowing in than out. The surplus is what we then save for the future. When we are either regularly experience neutral or worse, negative cash positions every month, we won't be able to save money for our future needs.

There are 2 ways to save regularly and irregularly. Saving regularly means we always set aside a portion of cash inflows as savings while saving irregularly is dependent on either a relatively bigger cash inflow, our mood swings or both. There are advantages and disadvantages to saving money either way.

One of the best advantages of saving regularly is that it becomes an automatic habit. It becomes normal. Also, it requires a lesser financial burden as regularly saving money usually requires smaller amounts than irregular ones just to become meaningful. The easier and more regular it is, the more successful we can be in terms of saving money.

A disadvantage of saving regularly, if you may even call it that, is we'll need a bigger cash inflow to meet our current needs regularly because a significant chunk of it may be taken by savings. A small price to pay, however.

An advantage to irregular savings is that we have more free money to spend. The disadvantage though, is that it's much harder to sustain compared to saving small and regular amounts of money. It's because saving money sporadically causes our savings muscles to atrophy, i.e., weaken our ability to save regularly. It also doesn't help that if we find it difficult to save small amounts of money, how much harder it would be to save much bigger amounts.

Case in point:

Month	Regular Savings Amount	Irregular Savings Amount
January	$1,000.00	
February	$1,000.00	
March	$1,000.00	$2,000.00
April	$1,000.00	
May	$1,000.00	
June	$1,000.00	
July	$1,000.00	$3,000.00
July	$1,000.00	
September	$1,000.00	

October	$1,000.00	
November	$1,000.00	
December	$1,000.00	$7,000.00
Total Savings For The Year	**$12,000.00**	**$12,000.00**

Which of the 2 do you think has a lower financial burden? I know, right? By saving smaller but regular amounts, you can successfully save and continue doing so even after you reached your desired amount.

THE TIME IS NOW

Yes, there's no other time to start saving than now. Why? The sooner you start, the lower your financial burden and the faster you can save up for the amount you have in mind. What makes this possible?

Compounding. Yes, the 8th wonder of the world per Einstein is what makes it possible. The earlier we start saving, the faster compounding can work in our favor.

BANKS

Banks are the best place to keep our savings. Why? Security is one good reason. Banks and their branches are built to maximize the protection of our money with fireproof and high tech vaults and security systems, it'll be hard for someone to just break in and rob the bank. But what if someone does manage to break in or rob it? No worries – banks are liable to pay you back for it.

Once we deposit our money with them, we transfer the risk to them.

What if the banks go, pardon the pun, bankrupt and close down? For many countries, bank deposits are insured with the government through one of their agencies. In the United States and Canada, there's the Federal Deposit Insurance Corporation (FDIC) and Canadian Deposit Insurance Corporation (CDIC), respectively.

Another reason why it's the best place to place our money is convenience. If we need to pay someone a huge amount, we don't have to carry all that cash and run the risk of getting robbed or losing the money along the way. We can either pay through checks or electronic fund transfers via the Internet or telephone without having to physically bring cash. For the top banks, we can directly invest our money directly from our bank accounts to wherever we want to invest via online banking.

Generally speaking, there are 3 types of bank accounts: savings, checking and time deposits. Savings accounts are the basic ATM or passbook based accounts that we can withdraw anytime through over-the-counter (passbook based) or through the ATM. Checking accounts are practically the same except that it doesn't have a passbook and withdrawals are generally made through checks that we issue. Banks give us checkbooks from which we can pay other people or institutions. Time deposits are deposit accounts that pay higher interest but in exchange, we can't withdraw our money until after a particular date, also called a maturity date, wherein we get back both the principal amount and interest. If we withdraw the money before then, we get "penalized" with a lower interest rate.

SAVING MONEY ISN'T ENOUGH

Saving money is definitely important in providing for our future needs but it isn't enough. We'll need to invest it to make it grow and work for us. When we save money, it doesn't work for us but when we invest it, our money starts working for us. In the next chapter, we'll discuss what investing is, how it's different from savings, why we need to invest the money we save and the different kinds of investments.

INVESTING

"How many millionaires do you know who have become wealthy by investing in savings accounts? I rest my case." – Robert G. Allen

This is one of the reasons why it isn't enough to save our money in the bank. With the very low interest rates banks pay on deposits, it'll take a million years before we can become millionaires. Or at least save enough money for future needs.

Investing is the act of committing financial resources with the expectation of a significant amount of profit or return. Investing has for its goal the opportunity to earn a nice enough profit commensurate to risks taken.

The common types of investments are stocks, debt papers, currencies, real estate and network marketing.

STOCKS

Stocks, or shares of stocks, are financial instruments that represent ownership of a company. The more stocks we buy, the more we own of the company. Stocks can be bought and sold in an organized exchange or market such as the New York Stock Exchange and Nasdaq or over-the-counter, the latter meaning we'll have to personally look for counterparties to transact with. To buy and sell stocks in organized exchanges, you'll have to go through stockbrokers that are members of a particular exchange.

There are 2 ways to earn from investing in stocks: capital appreciation and dividends. Capital appreciation is when the price or market value of our stock investments exceeds our purchase cost. We make money when we sell our stock investments at a higher price.

Dividends are our share of the profits of the company. The company's board of directors may declare dividends to be paid to shareholders as of a certain date when the company performed well according to expectations. During times that it doesn't no dividends are declared.

Capital appreciation is the best way to earn significant returns on stock investments while dividends usually aren't that meaningful. Most people who hit the gold mine in stock market investing did so via capital appreciation of their investments.

DEBT PAPERS

Debt papers are claims to money of other institutions, including the government. We primarily earn income on such investments through interest paid by the institutions that borrow our money.

Debt papers may be classified as either government securities or commercial papers. Government securities are debt papers issued by the government, which include treasury bills and treasury bonds. They can be issued either in the local currency or in a foreign one, such as US dollars or the Euro.

We can also make money through capital appreciation. This happens when interest rates go down, which makes the market value of debt papers higher. When interest rates go up, the market values of such papers go down. Interest rate movements are of no value when we invest in debt papers with the intention of holding on to them until they mature and only matters if we need to sell the papers, i.e., convert them back into cash, before maturity.

CURRENCIES

We can make money by buying and selling different currencies. Just like capital appreciation in stocks, we can earn money from changes in the currencies' prices or exchange rates.

Take for example the Japanese Yen (JPY). If the current exchange rate is JPY 120 per $US and we buy $1,000 worth of yen, we'll receive JPY 120,000. If the exchange rate changes to JPY 110 per $US, we can exchange our JPY for US$1,090.91, giving us a profit of $90.91.

REAL ESTATE

We can invest in real estate in 2 ways: leasing it or selling it. Leasing is a more consistent source of cash inflows but it will take longer for us to recoup our capital. Buying and selling real estate – also known in the United States as flipping properties – can help us recoup our investments much faster but it can tie up our cash flows for a longer period because selling properties take time and unlike leasing, doesn't provide for regular cash inflows.

One downside to real estate investing is that it's very capital intensive, i.e., requires a great amount of money unlike investing in stocks, debt papers and currencies. As such, the profits are also as handsome.

NETWORK MARKETING

Also known as multi-level marketing or MLM, network marketing is an investment that can provide multiple sources of cash inflows.

First is by selling the networking company's products, which we get at distributors' or wholesale prices, at retail prices. Second way is through commissions from recruiting people into the company. Lastly, we can earn from the sales and recruits of our recruits, also known as downlines. Many people get rich from the 3rd method because it's through it that they are effectively able to "multiply" themselves and their sales.

ACTIVE VS. PASSIVE INVESTMENTS

Active investments are those that require a great degree of active participation such as monitoring and management. Passive investments, on the other hand, require very little of such. Examples of active investments include stock market trading, currency trading, the initial stages of network marketing and flipping properties. Passive investing includes a buy-and-hold approach in the stock market, network marketing's latter stages and leasing properties.

Stock market trading is a short-term approach to investing wherein we immediately sell stocks as soon as we make a decent enough profit and buy again when prices dip significantly. Contrast this to what is known as a buy-and-hold approach, which is a passive form of investing. We simply buy stocks, forget about them and wait for them to increase in value over time. The potentially higher income that can be earned by actively trading has a tradeoff: close monitoring and management. It's because if we miss a major market movement, we can lose money. A buy-and-hold approach on the other hand, doesn't require much monitoring. Bulk of the work comes before buying because we'll need to choose stocks that have very good long-term potentials of capital appreciation.

Currency trading is basically active investing as most currencies go up and down within a relatively fixed price range and all we have to do is time our purchases and sales as it moves within such ranges to make profits. As with stock trading, we need to regularly monitor and manage our investments here as a quick and significant market movement can spell the difference between large profits or losses.

In network marketing, the biggest chunk of the work comes at the start – the first year or two – when we're just trying to build up our network and client base. Once we're able to do that, our clients start buying from us regardless if we sell to them or not and our network of recruits or downlines are already consistently selling and recruiting, both of which can provide us a great source of passive income with little to no active involvement. Some of my friends who are successfully into this tell me that active management for them is simply checking their bank accounts for commissions that are credited and withdrawing them.

When it comes to real estate investing, we can also do it actively or passively. Leasing our properties is closer to passive investing because there's very minimal management and monitoring needed while rental income is generally constant. Active management can be limited to just checking on the properties every now and then, contract renewal or looking for new tenants, all of which can be outsourced to a reliable and trustworthy real estate broker as my father-in-law does. Flipping properties do require more work from choosing the property to buy, processing the transfer of ownership, fixing or modifying said property, actively marketing it and processing transfer of ownership to the buyer.

RISK AND RETURN

There's one relationship that's central to successful investing: the higher is our expected return, the higher the risk we'll need to take. There's simply no getting around this relationship.

What is risk? It is simply the odds or the chances that something undesirable can happen. When it comes to investing, there are 3 kinds: market risk, credit risk and liquidity risk.

Market risk are the odds or chances that something undesirable – particularly financial losses – can happen because of the movements in the market prices of our investments. Trading stocks and currencies and to some extent, buying-and-holding stocks, are the kinds of investments that are most susceptible to this kind of risk.

When we buy a stock or a currency, there's a chance that its price will go down instead of up. When that happens, we initially incur what is called a paper loss, which is simply a "theoretical" one. As long as we continue holding on to the investment despite a drop in its price, we won't suffer the loss just yet. But when we sell at the lower price, the loss becomes real.

There's a flip side to holding on to a market-driven investment when prices have already gone down. Sure, we may not realize the loss but we run the risk of suffering a bigger one down the line if the prices of such investments continue to go down even further. Know your markets well and exercise great care and wisdom when trading stocks and currencies.

Consistent with the risk-return relationship, stocks and currencies are 2 investments where we can earn the highest possible returns given the relatively higher market risk compared to, say, bank deposits, debt papers or real estate investments.

Credit risk is the chance or possibility that we won't be able to get our money back. This type of risk is primarily associated with investments in debt papers and to some extent, leasing of properties. With debt papers, there is a chance that the institution we placed or lent our money to may not be able to pay us back. In terms of property rentals, there's a risk that our tenants may not be able to pay the rent.

Government-issued debt papers, particularly those denominated in the local currency, are practically credit-risk free and thus have the lowest interest rates among debt papers. Why? Governments have the sovereign power to print local money in the worst-case scenario that it becomes unable to pay local currency-denominated debts and so payment of such is practically assured. That's why in most countries, the interest rates on local currency denominated debt papers serve as the benchmark rates for commercial lendings and borrowings, where a certain amount of premium is added to compensate for the additional risk.

The last type of risk is liquidity risk, which is the possibility of not being able to liquidate or convert our investments back into cash on time when we need it. Investments with the highest liquidity risk are real estate investments because these are major investments that normally require a lot of money. Shares of stocks listed in major stock exchanges like the New York Stock Exchange and Nasdaq as well as major world currencies like the US$ have the lowest liquidity risk because they can easily be bought and sold.

HOW MUCH TO INVEST?

To answer this question, we need to consider several factors: investment goals, current market rates of return, risk tolerance and time frame. The primary consideration of course is our goal, i.e., how much money do we need for the future. Once we establish that, we can work back the amount we need to invest given our time frame and current market rates of return.

For example, we need $100,000.00 10 years from now. Further, if the expected average annual return for stocks, currencies, debt papers, property rentals and flipping properties is 20%, 15%, 10% and 30%, respectively, we the estimated amount of investment needed today based on the time value of money would be:

Investment	Expected Average Annual Return	Amount To Invest Now[2]
Stocks	20%	$16,150.56
Currencies	15%	$24,718.47
Debt Papers	4%	$67,556.42
Property Rentals	10%	$38,554.33
Flipping Properties	30%	$7,253.82

It's not just a matter of choosing the investment that will require the least amount of money to achieve $100,000 in ten years. We'll also need to consider the amount of risk we're willing to take. Flipping properties may require the least amount of money in our example but we'll have to consider its high liquidity risk and the amount of active involvement needed to make it work. Investing in stocks may have the lowest liquidity risk and active management requirement but it also has the highest market risk. Debt papers may have the lowest market risk and possibly a middle-of-the-pack level of liquidity risk but as such, it also requires the highest amount of investment because of its low returns.

At the end of the day, we should choose an investment that best matches our risk tolerance and financial capacity.

INFLATION BENCHMARKING

When it comes to investing, it's not enough to look at the expected rates of return. We also need to consider the inflation rate, which is the rate at which prices in general increase. For purposes of investing, we need to look at inflation from another perspective – the rate at which our money loses its purchasing power.

How's that so? If at the same time last year, apples cost $0.50 per piece and today it costs $0.55, our $1.00 can no longer purchase 2 apples. The increase in the price of apples (inflation) meant that the same amount of money today can no longer buy the same amount of apples compared to last year. Using this analogy, we can say that an inflation rate of 3% means our money lost 3% of its purchasing power.

Now what does this have to do with choosing investments? Everything. Remember that we invest our money to make it grow and allow us to meet future needs? Do you also remember that another reason we do it is because inflation causes the cost of our needs now to increase in the future? If we don't benchmark the expected returns of our potential investments against the prevailing and expected inflation rates, we may still end up losing money and fail to provide for our future needs.

When choosing potential investments, the expected return should exceed inflation by at least the rate of return required to meet our future needs. Let me explain this better.

Let's say that given the money that we have now, we need to invest at an average annual return of at least 10% for the next ten years to meet our projected financial need. If the average inflation rate for the last 10 years is 3%, we need an investment whose average expected annual return is at least 13%. Why? Because after we deduct inflation, we still have an expected average annual return of 10% (13% minus 3%). If the expected average annual return on an investment is less than inflation, we're actually going to lose money on it.

----

[2] Compounded annually.

PUTTING IT ALL TOGETHER

We all have needs and wants, which all require money. Personal finance is the ongoing activity of managing our money so that we can ensure that all our needs – both current and future ones – are met along with as much of our wants as possible.

Most people get by meeting their current needs and leave the future ones to fate. We shouldn't do that. We should prepare for them while we still have time. Personal finance management can go a long way in helping us prepare to meet our future needs like retirement or our children's college education.

The key to successful personal finance management is cash flow management, the results of which are either neutral cash flows (money going in and out are equal), negative (more money going out than coming in) and positive (more money coming in than going out). Positive cash flows are the key to being able to meet both current and future needs because it allows us to provide for current needs and save money for future needs.

Saving money for future needs, however, isn't enough because of inflation, or the rate of increase in the general cost of living. We need to grow our money at a much faster rate than inflation to be able to successfully provide for future needs. Investing is the way to do this.

Investing requires that we take risks: credit, market and liquidity. Credit risk is the possibility that we won't be able to get our money back. Market risk is the possibility of incurring losses due to changes in the market values of our investments. Liquidity risk is the risk that we won't be able to convert our investments back into cash on time when we need it. Expected returns are higher when we take on higher risks and vice versa.

Some of the most common investments include stocks, debt papers, currencies, network marketing and real estate. Investments can also be classified as to active and passive, the former requiring a lot of active involvement while the latter require very minimal involvement.

Choosing investments should take into consideration our investment objectives, risk tolerance, average expected rates of return, average inflation rate and time frame. For this, we'll need to carefully and wisely evaluate our investment alternatives.

When our cash flow management results in regular negative cash flows, we may fall into bad personal debts. We can, however, get out of it with enough discipline and financial wisdom to register regular positive cash flows.

Debts aren't necessarily bad, however. Handled well and responsibly, debts can actually aid us in managing our personal finances well and provide for future needs like a home. That being said however, it's best to avoid debts unless needed and the payment terms are affordable.

And that in a nutshell, is personal finance management.

APPENDICES:

Appendix A: Chapter 3, 10-Year Loan Compounded Quarterly At 10% per annum.

		Beginning Principal	Interest	Ending Principal
Year 1	1st Quarter	$10,000.00	$250.00	$10,250.00
	2nd Quarter	$10,250.00	$256.25	$10,506.25
	3rd Quarter	$10,506.25	$262.66	$10,768.91
	4th Quarter	$10,768.91	$269.22	$11,038.13
Year 2	1st Quarter	$11,038.13	$275.95	$11,314.08
	2nd Quarter	$11,314.08	$282.85	$11,596.93
	3rd Quarter	$11,596.93	$289.92	$11,886.86
	4th Quarter	$11,886.86	$297.17	$12,184.03
Year 3	1st Quarter	$12,184.03	$304.60	$12,488.63
	2nd Quarter	$12,488.63	$312.22	$12,800.85
	3rd Quarter	$12,800.85	$320.02	$13,120.87
	4th Quarter	$13,120.87	$328.02	$13,448.89
Year 4	1st Quarter	$13,448.89	$336.22	$13,785.11
	2nd Quarter	$13,785.11	$344.63	$14,129.74
	3rd Quarter	$14,129.74	$353.24	$14,482.98
	4th Quarter	$14,482.98	$362.07	$14,845.06
Year 5	1st Quarter	$14,845.06	$371.13	$15,216.18
	2nd Quarter	$15,216.18	$380.40	$15,596.59
	3rd Quarter	$15,596.59	$389.91	$15,986.50
	4th Quarter	$15,986.50	$399.66	$16,386.16
Year 6	1st Quarter	$16,386.16	$409.65	$16,795.82
	2nd Quarter	$16,795.82	$419.90	$17,215.71
	3rd Quarter	$17,215.71	$430.39	$17,646.11
	4th Quarter	$17,646.11	$441.15	$18,087.26

Year 7	1st Quarter	$18,087.26	$452.18	$18,539.44
	2nd Quarter	$18,539.44	$463.49	$19,002.93
	3rd Quarter	$19,002.93	$475.07	$19,478.00
	4th Quarter	$19,478.00	$486.95	$19,964.95
Year 8	1st Quarter	$19,964.95	$499.12	$20,464.07
	2nd Quarter	$20,464.07	$511.60	$20,975.68
	3rd Quarter	$20,975.68	$524.39	$21,500.07
	4th Quarter	$21,500.07	$537.50	$22,037.57
Year 9	1st Quarter	$22,037.57	$550.94	$22,588.51
	2nd Quarter	$22,588.51	$564.71	$23,153.22
	3rd Quarter	$23,153.22	$578.83	$23,732.05
	4th Quarter	$23,732.05	$593.30	$24,325.35
Year 10	1st Quarter	$24,325.35	$608.13	$24,933.49
	2nd Quarter	$24,933.49	$623.34	$25,556.82
	3rd Quarter	$25,556.82	$638.92	$26,195.74
	4th Quarter	$26,195.74	$654.89	$26,850.64
	Total Interest		$16,850.64	

Appendix B: Chapter 3, 10-Year Loan Compounded Annually At 10% per annum.

	Beginning Principal	Interest	Ending Principal
Year 1	$10,000.00	$1,000.00	$11,000.00
Year 2	$11,000.00	$1,100.00	$12,100.00
Year 3	$12,100.00	$1,210.00	$13,310.00
Year 4	$13,310.00	$1,331.00	$14,641.00
Year 5	$14,641.00	$1,464.10	$16,105.10
Year 6	$16,105.10	$1,610.51	$17,715.61
Year 7	$17,715.61	$1,771.56	$19,487.17
Year 8	$19,487.17	$1,948.72	$21,435.89
Year 9	$21,435.89	$2,143.59	$23,579.48
Year 10	$23,579.48	$2,357.95	$25,937.42
	Total Interest	$15,937.42	

Appendix C:

Lump Sum Payment

Principal	Interest Rate	Interest
$1,000.00	10.00%	$100.00

Quarterly Payments

Quarter	Initial Balance	Interest Rate[3]	Interest	Principal Payment	Ending Balance
1	$1,000.00	2.50%	$25.00	$250.00	$750.00
2	$750.00	2.50%	$18.75	$250.00	$500.00
3	$500.00	2.50%	$12.50	$250.00	$250.00
4	$250.00	2.50%	$6.25	$250.00	$0.00
Total Interest			$62.50		

Appendix D: Comparative Returns-On-Investment Using Debt

	Completely Funded By Owners' Money	50% Funded By Debt
Investment	$100,000.00	$50,000.00
Borrowed Money	$0.00	$50,000.00
Annual Revenue	$50,000.00	$50,000.00
Annual Interest On Borrowed Money (10%)	$0.00	$5,000.00
Business Expenses	$30,000.00	$30,000.00
Expenses And Interest	$30,000.00	$35,000.00
Net Income	$20,000.00	$15,000.00
Return On Investment (Net Income ÷ Investment)	20.00%	30.00%

Click here to go back

----

[3] Since payments are made every quarter, or 4 times a year, the interest rate per quarter is 10% ÷ 4 quarters or 2.5%.

PREVIEW OTHER BOOKS BY THIS AUTHOR

"Budgeting for Beginner's" by Craig Santoro

[Excerpt from the first 3 Chapters)

Living Paycheck to Paycheck

Are you tired of the constant feeling that you don't have any money? Living paycheck to paycheck is a real problem for many people. While some of the people in this rut are low earning families, many are not. Those in the middle class can also become entrenched in this cycle.

There is an old saying that you will spend what you earn. Generally it is expected that you are living within your means and meeting all of your financial obligations. At the same time, you don't have any money left over. As you earn more money you take on additional expenses or luxuries that eat up the additional income. This is how many families fall into the paycheck to paycheck cycle.

It is very possible to break this cycle. You have to have some willpower. You have to force yourself to deal with delayed gratification. Here are some tips for breaking the cycle.

The Importance of Curbing Spending

Most people who have trouble making ends meet or running out of money before the next paycheck hits actually spend quite a bit on unnecessary expenses. When you cut back on some of the luxuries of life you will find that you can save vast amounts of money. Even if it is something as simple as choosing an off brand at the grocery store, all of those pennies and dollars add up quickly. Here are a few ways you can curb your spending.

- Limit fast food trips to two per month
- Buy off brands at the grocery store
- Shop thrift stores for clothing before going to department stores
- Limit entertainment such as movies and concerts to one per month
- Cut out or cut down your cable or satellite bill
- Cut back on cell phone usage and bills
- Never use payday loans—they cost more than they're worth
- Cut back on driving to the bare minimum to save on gas
- Turn up the thermostat in the summer and down in the winter—dress for the weather instead of compensating with high energy bills
- Cut out or cut back on vices such as soda and cigarettes

- Make your own desserts instead of buying prepackaged cookies and cakes

These are just some of the ways you can trim the fat from your spending. Carefully consider where you spend money that you don't need to spend. Anything you can cut back would be beneficial. At the same time, don't deny yourself every pleasure. You have to feel like you are benefiting from your frugal lifestyle and all of your hard work. Denying yourself every luxury all the time will cause you to give up on budgeting.

The Importance of Saving for the Future

One of the biggest problems with living paycheck to paycheck is that you don't save back any money for the future. Whether you are looking five years ahead or thirty, it is important to save at least a small amount from each paycheck toward your long term goals.

Of course, the big savings goal many people think about is their retirement. If you are younger than 40, this event may seem so far in the future that it is hardly worth worrying about. However, this is the attitude that is leaving many middle aged adults struggling to figure out what they are going to do when they have to retire. Saving money for your retirement needs to start at a younger age. If you start early, you can save a large amount of money without hurting your average income and spending.

There are many other things that are closer to the present that you might want to save up for. If you are close to any of these events, or you just want to be prepared for them in the future, you should definitely start saving now. Here are just a few.

- A wedding for yourself or your child

- Preparing for a baby

- College tuition for a child

- A car that you don't have to make payments on

- A down payment on a house that will save you on housing costs

- A nest egg for maintenance or replacement of major appliances as they age

- A family vacation that your children will remember for a lifetime

Saving money isn't just about surviving. It's about living. Without saving back money for the little things, and the big things, that come along in life, you will fail to truly enjoy them when they arrive because you will be struggling to pay for them. Planning ahead not only keeps you prepared for emergencies, but also decreases stress and increases overall happiness.

How Budgeting Helps You Meet Your Goals

Budgeting is an important step in helping you meet your goals. Budgeting isn't just about being careful with your money. You can use budgeting tools to help you plan your income and spending so that you can intentionally set aside savings. You can use expense tracking to help you trim the fat from your budget and see where you can make changes to improve your overall quality of life, now and in the future. Your long term financial goals, as well as your short term way of life, can only be realized through effective budgeting.

Methods of Budgeting

There are three primary ways to budget. You can budget by week or pay period, month, or by expense. Budgeting by expense is the easiest way to budget. It is generally done by using the envelope method, which will be explained shortly. Budgeting by week or pay period can help you stop the paycheck to paycheck cycle, but works with that mentality while you work to improve your financial habits. Monthly budgeting is helpful because you can see everything you spend monthly at one time. This is important because many bills are only paid once per month.

You may choose to use a combination of methods. Sometimes it can be helpful to have even the most basic monthly budget to use in combination with a weekly budget. It can also help to use the envelope method, especially if you have difficulty setting aside money for larger expenses.

Budgeting Basics

Regardless of what method you use to budget, you will need to understand some basic concepts that must be used. These tools and concepts are vitally important to your budgeting success. They should be used diligently, especially when you are just starting out. You will need to use the information from these tools to help you create effective and accurate budgets.

Tracking Income

There are some important things to keep in mind when tracking income. You want your budget to be as accurate as possible. If you overestimate how much income you will have you could throw your entire budget off balance. You could wind up short for the week or month, and be unable to pay an important bill.

When you consider your income for your budget you should calculate all *reliable* sources of income. This means that you need to incorporate only that income which is guaranteed. This is usually your paycheck. When you calculate the money you will have, don't use your gross pay. If you work the same number of hours per week you can use the net pay from your check stubs to see what you can budget for income. If your work hours vary, calculate your gross income and deduct 25% for taxes. You may have fewer deductions than that, but it is better to be safe than sorry.

You may have other sources of income such as that from a side job, child support or alimony. If you have steady income from one or more of these sources that is guaranteed, feel free to add it to your budgeted income. Guaranteed income is income that is received on a scheduled basis. It also must be received with continuity, such as on time each period for at least three to six months.

If you have a child support or alimony order but the money doesn't always come on time or at all, you should not count it as income in your budget. If you budget for this income and then it doesn't show up it will throw your entire financial plan out of whack and you will have to face potentially serious consequences.

Tracking Expenses

There are many ways that you can track your expenses and spending. Tracking expenses is especially important when you first start budgeting. It is vital that you know where all of your money is going. Creating a budget of what you anticipate spending is an important aspect of your budget. But tracking expenses tells you where your money is actually going.

Tracking expenses is important because it helps you determine what you need to budget for. Bills like rent and a car payment are fixed expenses that you don't really have to think about. But most expenses are variable, meaning that they are different each month. The only way to budget for variable expenses is to have some idea of what that amount might be.

It is pretty easy to track your expenses. You can easily create a spreadsheet on your computer where you can enter your expenses daily and have a monthly total running at the bottom. There are such spreadsheets available online as well. This requires keeping receipts and entering each expense.

You can also get expense trackers on your smart phone with many different available apps. This is helpful for making sure that you don't miss any expenses when you enter them into your tracking at home. If you are single you can just use the expense tracker app. If you have a significant other you will need to combine your tracking and theirs on a master spreadsheet or software.

Budgeting for Variable Expenses

This is where your expense tracker will come in handy. When you track your spending for the previous month you can use that information to help you budget for your variable expenses for the following month. As you continue this trend you can calculate the average spending for that item based on several months of data. This will give you the most accurate budget possible.

It is important that you give yourself some leeway when it comes to variable expenses. You should always pad them, even if just by a few dollars, when doing your budget. This way you will not run into serious problems if the expense ends up being a bit more than you thought. If you have extra money at the end of the budget period because you padded your variable expenses you can use that money to help make larger purchases that you couldn't afford before, or you can add it to your savings nest egg.

It is best to budget as closely as possible. As already mentioned your expense tracker can help you with some of that. Past spending habits can help you calculate the budget for things like gasoline, food and household items. Some variable expenses require a different tactic.

For utility bills, for example, you will want to look back at your previous bills for the current season. In other words, if it is summer you need to look back to see what the average bill was in the previous summer. This can usually be done by contacting your utility company and requesting the information. If this is your first season in your home you can still contact the utility company and they will give you average utility costs for that month in the previous year based on the previous resident's usage.

Grocery Budget Tips

Budgeting for groceries is perhaps one of the most difficult variable expenses to calculate. Food prices vary greatly. Sometimes you can get great deals and catch awesome sales, and sometimes you will have to pay full price no matter where in the city you go to shop. Meat prices rise and fall. Any number of things can change the price of food with little or no notice.

Your previous spending will give you a starting point for your grocery budget. Look back through several months of spending to get an idea of the average amount you spend. Try to go with the higher number just to make sure that you have enough budgeted.

It also helps to make a meal plan for the budget period, make a grocery list, and estimate the amount of money you will spend to fulfill that list. Again, pad the budget a bit to make sure you have enough money for groceries in case prices rise or something unexpected comes up.

There is one great tool that you can use to help you make your grocery budget more accurate. You can build a spreadsheet for it. There are also a few apps and websites that will help you do this. You have to track every item that you buy. You bring home your grocery receipt and input the store, date, item, size, and price. By doing this you will be able to see exactly what you pay for each item.

When you create a meal plan for the next budget period you can look back at your itemized list and see what you paid for each item. Your grocery list will be made and you will have an almost exact dollar amount of what you will spend. Not everyone has the time to do this, but if you can it is a great tool that can really help you.

The Envelope Method

The envelope method is the simplest way to budget. This is the method that has been taught to young people for years before budgeting software and apps were commonplace. All you need are some regular mailing envelopes and somewhere safe to keep them.

Why It Works

The envelope method works well for people who need to visually see what they need to pay and where their money is going. It is also a great way to budget if you aren't good with computers or number crunching. Budgeting using envelopes also works extremely well for people who pay using cash.

If you don't have a checking account or prefer to work with cash then envelope budgeting is extremely helpful. It allows you to set aside money so that it isn't just sitting in your wallet. This way you don't spend money that you need for a particular expense.

The Process

To use the envelope method you will need to have some mailing envelopes and a safe place to store them. A fire safe is fairly inexpensive. You can get a small one for around $50. Not only will having your money stored out of sight help you keep from spending it, it will also help keep it from being stolen.

You will need to first determine your most basic expenses that you need to budget for. Make a list of every type of expense you will have throughout the month. You will then create an envelope for each expense on your list. Here is an example list:

- Rent
- Electric bill
- Gas bill
- Water bill
- Phone bill
- Car payment
- Gasoline
- Groceries
- Household items
- Dining and Entertainment

If you don't have a savings account you may also want to make a list of savings goals. You would then have an envelope for each of those as well.

These are usually short term savings goals such as:

- Buying new tires for your car
- Buying a computer, television or other big ticket item
- Buying needed furniture or beds

- Buying needed clothing

- Saving for an anticipated move

- Fund for unexpected car maintenance

- Fun for other unexpected expenses

On each envelope write the name of the expense and the amount you need to put into the envelope each month. For savings envelopes write the total amount you want to save for that item. Number your savings envelopes in order of priority.

When you get money you will divide it into your necessary envelopes. Start with the most important expenses such as rent, utilities and groceries. If you drive your car payment and gasoline will need to come next. Save non-essential expenses for last. Once all of your expense envelopes have the correct amount in them you can begin dividing the rest into your savings envelopes.

It is likely that you get paid more than once per month, but most of your bills will be paid only once per month. It is best if you pay all of your bills at the first of the month. In order to do this you will need to put some money aside each paycheck to each monthly bill. Then at the beginning of the month you will have the money you need to pay each of your bills. Examples of monthly bills are rent and utilities.

Your variable expenses that occur throughout the month on an almost daily basis will be handled a bit differently. After you have put money aside in the monthly bill envelopes you will place money into your variable expense envelopes. Make sure that you have the minimum amount for your pay period in the envelopes. For example, you may have budgeted $400 for groceries for the month. If you get paid weekly you would put $100 per week into the envelope.

As you proceed through the month, use the money in each envelope only for that expense to which it is dedicated. If you really want to go out to eat but your dining envelope is empty, don't take money out of the grocery envelope to satisfy your craving. It is important that you only use the money for what it has been set aside.

Gauging Success

The envelope method doesn't really use precise expense tracking. You don't record each purchase or figure out exactly what you spent the money on. Instead, your success is gauged by what is left in your envelopes and if you have met all of your responsibilities for the month.

If your savings envelopes are gradually increasing then you know you are doing a great job. The more money you are able to save the more clear it is 3that you are staying within your budget.

There are also signs that you are not succeeding. For example, you could run out of money in your grocery envelope before your next paycheck. When this happens it could pay to track your spending in that area a bit more closely to make sure you aren't overspending. Maybe you should buy more veggies and fewer meats to save money.